# Table of Contents

Map Symbols     3

Photo Glossary     15

Index     16

About the Author     16

Rourke
Educational Media
rourkeeducationalmedia.com

MW00562245

# Can you find these words?

## city

## key

## river

## symbols

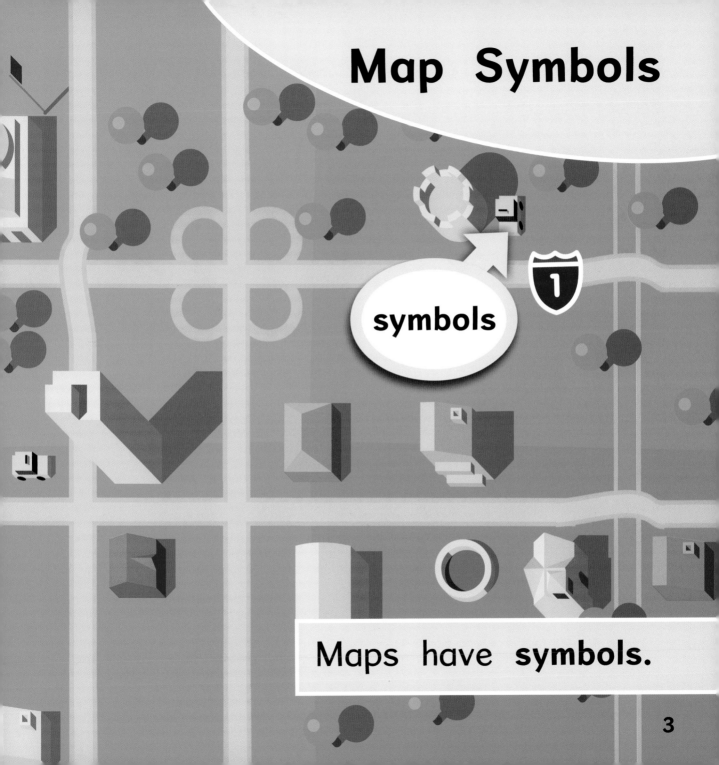

# Map Symbols

symbols

Maps have **symbols.**

# Symbols may be pictures, lines, colors, or dots.

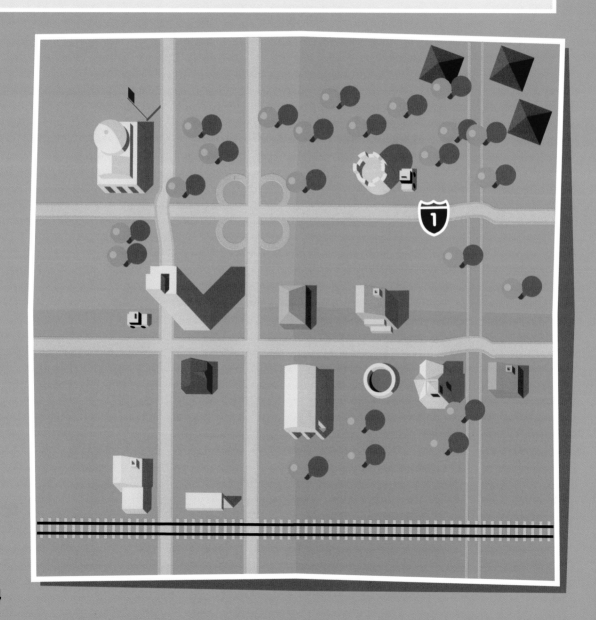

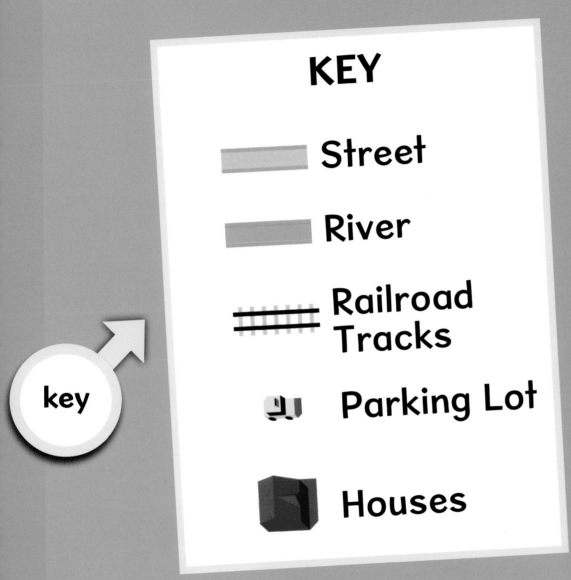

# KEY

Street

River

Railroad Tracks

Parking Lot

Houses

key

The **key** shows the map symbols.

Symbols stand for bigger things, like mountains, streets, or buildings.

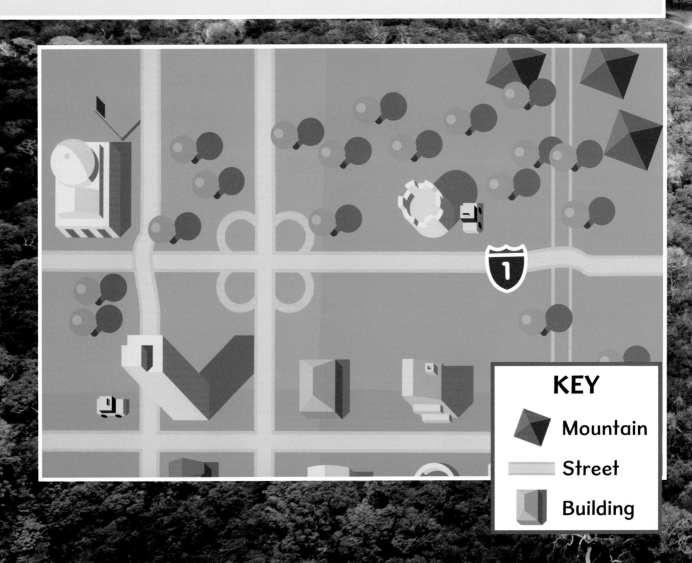

**KEY**

Mountain

Street

Building

A blue line might be a symbol for a **river**.

river

KEY
- • City
- — Street
- — River
- ✈ Airport

A tiny dot might be a symbol for a **city**.

city

**KEY**

Parking Lot

Street

River

A car might be a symbol for a parking lot.

# Can you find the school?

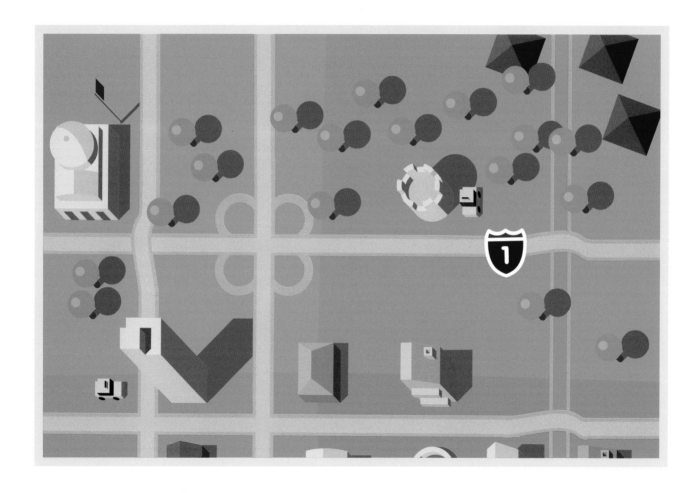

**KEY**

Street

River

Park

School

# Did you find these words?

A tiny dot might be a symbol for a **city**.

The **key** shows the map symbols.

A blue line might be a symbol for a **river**.

Maps have **symbols**.

# Photo Glossary

 **city** (SIT-ee): A very large or important town.

 **key** (kee): A list or chart that explains the symbols on a map.

 **river** (RIV-ur): A large, natural stream of fresh water that flows into a lake, an ocean, or another river.

 **symbols** (SIM-bulz): Objects that stand for, suggest, or represent something else.

# Index

buildings  6

car  11

map(s)  3, 5

mountains  6

school  12, 13

streets  6

# About the Author

Terri Fields likes reading with and writing for children. When she's not reading or writing, she likes walking on the beach.

www.rourkeeducationalmedia.com

PHOTO CREDITS: Cover: ©mikanaka; p. 2,8,14,15: ©Sean Pavone; p. 2,6,14,15: ©prasit chansarekorn; p. 4: ©exi5; p. 8: ©Günay Mutlu; p. 10: ©tomwald.

Edited by: Keli Sipperley
Cover design by: Kathy Walsh
Interior design by: Rhea Magaro-Wallace

**Library of Congress PCN Data**
Map Symbols / Terri Fields
(Let's Find Out)
ISBN (hard cover)(alk. paper) 978-1-64156-193-8
ISBN (soft cover) 978-1-64156-249-2
ISBN (e-Book) 978-1-64156-299-7
Library of Congress Control Number: 2017957803

Printed in the United States of America, North Mankato, Minnesota